Made in the USA
Columbia, SC
13 July 2025

60678053R00074